NATURE STYLE

A NATURAL HOME BOOK

NATURE STYLE

Elegant Decorating with Leaves, Twigs & Stones

Marthe Le Van

LARK BOOKS

A Division of Sterling Publishing Co., Inc.
New York

Art Direction: DANA IRWIN
Photography: KEITH WRIGHT
Cover Design: BARBARA ZARETSKY
Illustrations: SUSAN MCBRIDE
Contributing Editor: VALERIE SHRADER
Assistant Editors: VERONIKA ALICE GUNTER,
RAIN NEWCOMB
Assistant Art Director: HANNES CHAREN
Editorial Assistance: DANA LADE
Proofreader: SHERRY HAMES

Special Photography:
Roland Fischer, 91; Sandra Stambaugh, 6, 11, 49, 88, 89, 111;
Dana Irwin, 6, 7, 48, 88,110

Sanoma Syndication:
Henk Brandsen, 81, 107; Dennis Brandsma, 98, 99, 101, 118,
139; Frank Brandwijk, 36, 65; Bart Brussee, 129; Renneé
Frinking, 137; Rene Gonkel, 33, 91; Paul Grootes, 97, 131,
132, 135; Fons Klappe, 53; Peter Kooijman, 75, 117; Louis
Lemaire, 93; Ank Neumann, 94, 95; Harold Pereira, 60; Otto
Polman, 28, 29, 105; Dolf Straatemeier, 35, 69, 103, 119;
Alexander van Berge, 115; Jeroen van der Speck, 67; George
v.d. Wijngaard, 17, 23, 41, 42, 43, 44, 46, 47, 60, 61, 79, 85,
87, 113; John van Groenedaal, 133; Eric van Lokven, 59; Pia
van Spaendonck, 76, 77; Hans Zeegers, 121

Library of Congress has cataloged the hardcover edition as follows:

Le Van, Marthe.
    Nature style : elegant decorating with leaves, twigs & stones / Marthe Le Van.
        p. cm.
    Includes index.
    ISBN 1-57990-337-1
    1. Nature craft. 2. Interior decoration. 3. House furnishings. I. Title.

TT857 .L428 2002
747'.9--dc21

                                        2002020207

10 9 8 7 6 5 4 3 2 1

Published by Lark Books, a division of
Sterling Publishing Co., Inc.
387 Park Avenue South, New York, N.Y. 10016

First Paperback Edition 2004
© 2002, Lark Books

Distributed in Canada by Sterling Publishing,
c/o Canadian Manda Group, One Atlantic Ave., Suite 105
Toronto, Ontario, Canada M6K 3E7

Distributed in the U.K. by: Guild of Master Craftsman Publications Ltd.
Castle Place 166 High Street
Lewes East Sussex England BN7 1XU
Tel: (+ 44) 1273 477374
Fax: (+ 44) 1273 478606
Email: pubs@thegmcgroup.com Web: www.gmcpublications.com

Distributed in Australia by Capricorn Link (Australia) Pty Ltd., P.O. Box 704,
Windsor, NSW 2756 Australia

If you have questions or comments about this book, please contact:
Lark Books
67 Broadway
Asheville, NC 28801
(828) 253-0467

Printed in China
ISBN 1-57990-337-1 (hardcover) 1-57990-517-x (paperback)

CONTENTS

INTRODUCTION

I love the shocking intensity of yellow-green spring leaves, bursting forth to awaken my hibernating spirit. I love the way smooth water-worn stones caress the soles of my feet as I rock hop in a summer stream. I love autumn's kaleidoscope of color, when leaves appear to have been painted overnight. I love staring at the stark silhouettes of bare tree branches against a white winter sky.

A lifelong collector, I love bringing home mementos from these special times. In this book, I'd like to share many simple, imaginative, and tasteful ways to welcome leaves, twigs, and stones into your home so you can experience their essence and artfulness everyday.

We'll start with some basic information on collecting natural materials. Your most important practice, one that can not be stressed enough, is to be a responsible forager. Respect the environment wherever you roam. Observe all regulations against removing property from protected lands. This also applies to the stunning leaves on your neighbor's maple tree. In your own backyard, you're free to scavenge at will. Just remember to handle the elements in your landscape with care. Read up on pruning before trimming a twig, and consider drainage prior to removing garden stones.

Once you're well stocked with fresh leaves, twigs, and stones, refer to our tips for pressing leaves, washing stones, and checking twigs for bugs. Our natural decorating projects require few, if any, tools and materials. I'd venture to say that even the most reluctant do-it-yourselfer has most of the necessary items on hand.

The first section of the book, Natural Beauty, offers decorating projects and ideas that present leaves, twigs, and stones in their natural state. These objects convey an astonishing beauty that needs little enhancement; merely creating a modest arrangement is often enough. We've come up with some innovative locations for placing your leaves, twigs, and stones. Whether you contain them in a simple bowl or basket, loosely scatter them on a shelf, pin them to a wall, or stack them in the fireplace, these earthy accents will give you refreshing pause. We'll give you some basic principles for creating attractive tabletop displays. You can follow these suggestions to heighten the visual impact of your natural compositions. Appraising the color, texture, and dimension of objects, then sensing when to blend or contrast them with their surroundings will lead you to create dynamic designs.

After observing the sheer beauty of unaltered leaves, twigs, and stones, we'll then explore ways to make them functional. The Form and Function chapter is brimming with ideas for giving your home natural style. Whatever your decorating tastes, these handsome projects will fit into any interior scheme. Leaves, twig, and stones are as attractive on top of a contemporary chrome mantle as they are on a rustic wood end table. They bring as much life to a dark cozy living room as a white-washed bath. And, if you're looking to create a special dining experience, we've got that covered with plenty of natural embellishments to make your table the toast of the town.

The third chapter is dedicated to those of you with blank walls begging for attention. In On the Wall, we've designed artful arrangements of leaves, twigs, and stones that are meant to be hung. Some are gallery-quality works of art, such as Pebble Painting, on page 96, while others are organic framing ideas, such as Branching Out, on page 100. Although the wall projects are intended to be major focal points, their grace and understated elegance are in tune with nature's gentle spirit.

Holidays and special occasions are the focus of the final decorating chapter, Time to Celebrate. Following the calendar from season to season, we praise nature's glory in bold, striking forms. Because of their festive nature, many of these projects make spectacular party decorations, and they're so attractive, you might just find yourself leaving them up long after the revelry.

Sprinkled throughout the book are special interest sections. From all around the globe, we've collected some unusual legends and traditions with leaves, twigs, and stones as their central theme. These tales reflect nature's tremendous role in the cultural heritage and mythology of the earth's people. You'll also find examples of splendid artworks created from natural materials. These artists exhibit a profound respect for their materials and employ them with great sensitivity. I hope you'll find inspiration in their images.

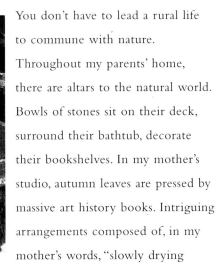

You don't have to lead a rural life to commune with nature. Throughout my parents' home, there are altars to the natural world. Bowls of stones sit on their deck, surround their bathtub, decorate their bookshelves. In my mother's studio, autumn leaves are pressed by massive art history books. Intriguing arrangements composed of, in my mother's words, "slowly drying things," fill every vase in the house. It was in this environment and through my parents' example that my eyes and soul opened to nature's unrivaled and sublime style. I hope you'll follow their lead, and discover the affluence of nature with innocent wonder and unbridled enthusiasm.

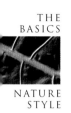

THE BASICS

SPECIAL INGREDIENTS

One of the most gratifying aspects of decorating with natural materials is the individuality and intimacy of the raw materials. Whether you undertake a simple or intricate design, your results will be like no other on earth. Every leaf, twig, and stone you collect is unique not only in its looks and history, but also in its relation to you, the collector. These materials are lasting reminders of a certain time in your life, places you have known, or people you hold dear.

COLLECTING LEAVES

Taking a walk is an entertaining and invigorating elixir to the stress and sensory bombardment of everyday life. On your next stroll, why not get some fresh leaves as well as fresh air? Pack a small journal or sketchbook, and slip your gathered leaves between its pages while you walk. Whether you follow a familiar neighborhood route, park path, or hiking trail, you're bound to spot beautiful leaves year round.

From smooth and round to jagged and angular, leaves come in all sorts of eye-catching shapes and sizes. Each tree species can be identified by its unique leaf design. It's helpful to have many different shapes and colors to work with, so try to collect an assortment of leaves from a variety of trees. In early autumn, it's tempting to overlook lovely green leaves in favor of those showing dramatic color, but green leaves will provide dynamic contrast in many displays. Pay close attention both to leaves on the ground and those still attached to branches. Always ask permission to harvest leaves off trees that are on private property, and refrain from selecting leaves that show signs of mold or rot.

COLLECTING TWIGS

Since there are more trees on earth than people, it's surprising that more people aren't fascinated by the attractive features of twigs. Case in point: there are vast artistic resources waiting to be discovered in people's yard waste. I often rummage (with the owner's permission, of course) through piles of twigs collected on the side of the road hoping to uncover an aesthetic jewel, or a specific type of wood. Since most twig stacks come from freshly pruned trees and shrubs, decay and insect damage are less of a problem. After raiding a brush pile, remember to be a responsible citizen and restack the wood before you leave. If you plan to cut twigs for your decorating ideas and projects, use proper pruning techniques so as not to damage the tree.

Different twigs have different working traits, or qualities that affect their use, such as strength, weight, and flexibility. Keep this in mind as you select the wood to use for your project. Though native woods vary from region to region, there are workable species in every zone. Birch, dogwood, elm, hemlock, silver maple, sycamore, and willow trees provide fine wood for twig projects. Large grapevines are also a good option. Wood shrinks as it dries and may warp or twist in the process. For this reason, dry your wood before building your project. Pine tree wood contains sap and is slow to dry, making it less than an ideal material.

When selecting twigs to bring into your home, make sure they aren't dead or rotten. One simple test is to bend the twig. If it crushes or breaks easily or feels soft and has a damp, mildewy smell, leave it for the bugs. They'll enjoy it for a sumptuous meal or as building material for a new home.

COLLECTING VINES

Vines require support to grow, so they climb by tendrils or twining, or creep along the ground. You can find vines growing along fence rows, roadsides, and in the woods. Woody-stemmed vines are the best variety for crafting, and they're easiest to use when fresh. Vines go dormant in the late fall, becoming harder to bend. You can improve their pliability by soaking them in water overnight. Honeysuckle, autumn clematis, kudzu, bittersweet, and virginia creeper are excellent choices. Grapevine shouldn't be trimmed for use unless you know the correct technique.

COLLECTING STONES

Your affinity for stones may have begun as a child, when you casually pocketed keepsakes from the playground, and continues to this day as you mindfully choose just the right memento of your travels. These activities are curiously instinctive. Perhaps it's because stones, even the backyard variety, are enchanting and powerful markers of time and place.

Different types of stones naturally occur in different geological regions. You'll find smooth, round stones near moving water, whereas sharp and flat stones are found in locations that are largely dry. Wherever you roam, be on the lookout for stones with character.

There are many places to shop for stones. Masonry yards, home-building and improvement centers, and craft and floral supply retailers offer a great diversity. The advantage of buying stones is that you can acquire similar sizes and colors in large quantities, and receive knowledgeable assistance from professionals. Masonry facilities offer additional services such as drilling, sawing, and installation advice.

Once you have your stones at home, rinse them in warm water to remove surface debris. If necessary, use a kitchen scrub brush to eliminate stubborn dirt. When the stones are wet, you'll notice that their colors and patterns look more intense. To maintain this sheen, polish your stones with a light, even coat of vegetable oil or jeweler's polish. To create an even higher gloss, you can polish the stones in a lapidary tumbler.

9

TOOLS & MATERIALS

The projects in this book are based on simple ideas, and are easy to make. You won't need any special technical knowledge or uncommon tools to accomplish the designs. Here are brief explanations of some of the most useful tools and materials when working with leaves, twigs, and stones.

TWIG TRIMMERS & SHAPERS

Hand pruners are like heavy-duty scissors for the garden with one blade overlapping the other. They're the perfect tool for trimming twigs and shrubs. A good pair of pruners should be lightweight, feel comfortable in your hand, cut cleanly, and operate easily. Use a pruning or shortcut saw for cutting small to medium green or woody branches off trees, shortening branch lengths, leveling bases, or making mitered cuts.

FLORAL FOAM

If you need to hold plant materials in place, plastic floral foam is the most versatile and convenient substance to use. It comes in both wet and dry varieties. Wet floral foam is used for fresh flowers and foliage because it absorbs and holds water. Because of its very fine consistency, wet floral foam easily supports delicate stems. Dry floral foam is made to use with dried materials. It's similar to wet floral foam, just slightly firmer. Both types of foams can be cut with a sharp knife into any desired shape.

FLORAL PINS

These U-shape pieces of wire look and work like hairpins. To use a floral pin, simply arrange the foliage or other material you wish to attach against a receptive base, such as foam. Position the pin with its prongs on either side of the material, and press the pin into the base at an angle.

FLORAL TAPE

Floral tape comes in several camouflaging shades of brown and green that are suitable for natural materials. Gently stretch the floral tape as you work to increase its adhesive quality.

FLORAL TUBES

These plastic tubes hold water and are capped with lids that have narrow slits for inserting fresh-cut leaves and flowers. The bottom of the tube comes to a long narrow point so that it can be inserted into a wreath base or other receptive surface.

FLORAL WIRE

Floral wire is one of those inexpensive, invaluable tools every decorator should keep around the house. Floral wire is sold in pre-cut lengths and on spools in a variety of thicknesses (referred to as *gauge*) and colors (brown, green, and silver). Although floral wire's connection is strong, it isn't permanent, and this can be a great advantage. Affixing with floral wire instead of an adhesive permits you to make adjustments to a design both from moment to moment and season to season.

BINDING

Leather lacing, synthetic sinew, waxed thread, ribbons, and cords make practical and attractive connectors for leaves, twigs, and stones. Raffia, a natural product derived from the fronds of the raffia palm of Madagascar, is also useful. It's sold at craft and floral supply stores in bundles, hanks, and bales in plain and dyed colors.

WIRE

Aluminum wire is soft, and therefore easy to twist around stones, twigs, and other decorations. Its dull metallic finish has a quiet coolness that complements natural materials. Copper wire is a warm-colored alternative that is also available in many gauges. Although wire can be trimmed with regular pliers, you may want to invest in an inexpensive, all-purpose pair of wire cutters.

PLIERS

Round-nose pliers, or jewelry pliers, are indispensable for creating decorative wire work and hanging loops for your projects. Needle-nose pliers act like skinny and strong finger extensions, allowing you to maneuver in and out of difficult places. This is particularly helpful when you're threading, weaving, and twisting wire. General purpose pliers are the type you'll find in most tool boxes. They have serrated jaws and a powerful gripping ability but are often too coarse for decorative work.

MISCELLANEOUS CRAFT SUPPLIES

These fundamental craft supplies are always good to have on hand: scissors, staple gun, hammer and nails, work gloves, candle or museum wax, wood glue, all-purpose heavy-duty epoxy, and measuring tape or stick.

PRESERVING LEAVES

No doubt you've collected a fantastic array of leaves on your walk. Now it's time to preserve their natural beauty. All types of leaves can be pressed, dried, or conserved in some manner. For the best results, work with your leaves immediately after their collection.

PRESSING

Healthy, fresh leaves are full of moisture. Place a sheet of absorbent paper in the center of a heavy

book; arrange a single layer of leaves on the paper; and place a second sheet on top. (Using an absorbent material such as paper towels or newspaper will help draw out moisture from the leaves before they have a chance to mold, and help protect the pages of your book.) Close the book, weighing it down if desired, and store it in a secluded area for at least 10 days to two weeks. If possible, change the absorbent paper after the first two days of pressing.

MICROWAVING

If pressing leaves doesn't suit your schedule, there are ways to speed the process. With practice, you can use a microwave oven to dry leaves in minutes, but, regrettably, there are no hard-and-fast guidelines to follow. Many factors will influence your microwave-drying success, such as oven wattage, power settings, and cooking times; the life-cycle stage of the harvested leaf; its moisture content, size and thickness; and the number of leaves being dried at one time.

Place a few leaves in an ordinary brown paper lunch bag, and gently fold up the open end. Put the bag on top of a microwave-safe bowl. (The bowl will catch any accumulating moisture that flows downward.) Start microwaving with a low time and wattage setting (about 1½ minutes on 50% power), adding extra time in small increments. Leaves continue to "cook" after microwaving, so allow for a few minutes of standing time with the end of the paper bag unrolled. Leaves that curl after microwaving are not dry enough, whereas scorched leaves are cooked too long. Keeping a notebook with detailed success and failure notes can save you from future frustrations.

BRILLIANT FALL COLOR

Each autumn, nature hosts a spectacular party, inviting everyone to marvel at her glorious colors. In response to shorter days and cooler nights, millions of trees in deciduous forests get ready for their dormant winter period. Their leaves are too vulnerable to survive a cold winter, so they're slowly shed, turning spectacular colors before falling.

The best fall leaf color comes when the weather is clear and dry with evening temperatures a bit chilly, but not below freezing. Many types of trees change colors at slightly different times over a period of three to four weeks.

Certain leaf colors are characteristic of a particular species of trees. In the fall, you'll see: aspen, birch, and yellow-poplar trees turn golden yellow; beech trees turn light tan; black maple trees turn glowing yellow; dogwood trees turn purplish red; hickory trees turn golden bronze; oak trees turn red, brown, or russet; red maple trees turn brilliant scarlet; sourwood and black tupelo trees turn crimson; and sugar maple trees turn orange-red.

SILICA GEL

Leaves also can be dried in the microwave with silica gel crystals, a moisture-absorbing substance sold in craft stores. To dry leaves in the microwave with silica gel crystals, first line the bottom of a microwave-safe container with a 1-inch-thick (2.5 cm) layer of crystals. Arrange the leaves on top, allowing about 1 inch of space around the sides and between each leaf. Cover with another 1-inch-thick (2.5 cm) layer of crystals, and then microwave on 50% power for three minutes. Check the leaves' progress, and add more time in short increments as needed. Always read and follow the manufacturer's safety precautions when using silica gel crystals.

GLYCERINE & WATER

Yet another way to preserve leaves is to immerse them in a mixture of glycerin and water. Glycerin, which is available at most pharmacies, preserves leaves without flattening them. This technique works best on freshly picked sturdy specimens such as holly, magnolia, and some maple. Make a solution of one part glycerin to two parts boiling water, and pour it into a flat pan. Submerge the leaves in the liquid, spreading them apart into a single layer. Store the pan in a secluded area for two to six days, and then take the leaves out of the pan and wipe off the solution with a soft cloth. Glycerine-treated leaves will remain soft and pliable indefinitely.

You can also use a glycerine and water solution to preserve twigs with attached leaves. Immerse the entire branch in a warm solution of one part glycerin to one part boiling water. Leave the branch in the mixture for at least double the time required to preserve a single leaf.

THE BUDDHA'S TREES

Many of the pivotal events in the Buddha's life involved trees. They're intimately connected with the two most important moments in his life—his birth and his enlightenment.

The Buddha's mother, Queen Maya, was traveling to her home to give birth, as was the custom of the day. Captivated by the beauty of Lumbini Park, Queen Maya asked her attendants to stop, and she grasped a branch of the sala tree. When she touched one of the lovely flowers, some legends say that the Buddha was born. Depictions of this event almost always show Queen Maya standing, one arm around a sala tree.

As a young man, the Buddha spent six faithful but fruitless years of self-denial searching for wisdom. Finally, he sat in meditation under the shelter of a pipal tree, and he reached enlightenment. For a week, he gazed at the tree in gratitude. Now, the pipal is called a bodhi, "the tree of awakening." Accordingly, it is the custom of Buddhists to pay respect to all bodhi trees.

Modern-day Buddhists have sanctified the Buddha's connection to trees. In 1997, Buddhist monks in Thailand ordained their forests to prevent clearcutting. The monks blessed the trees and tied orange scarves around their trunks; then, Buddhists who were working as loggers refused to cut the Buddha's trees.

NATURAL BEAUTY

SOMETIMES THE MOST ARTFUL ACT IS SIMPLY RECOGNIZING A GOOD THING AND LEAVING IT ALONE. THE IDEAS AND PROJECTS IN THIS SECTION CELEBRATE THE INTRINSIC BEAUTY OF THE ELEMENTS WITHOUT ALTERING THEIR ORGANIC FORMS. WHETHER IT'S A WATER-WORN RIVER STONE, A TAWNY WILLOW TWIG, OR AN EYE-CATCHING AUTUMN LEAF, EACH COMPONENT IS A UNIQUE GIFT FROM NATURE THAT IS READY TO TAKE CENTER STAGE IN YOUR HOME.

BIRCH RUNNER

Table runners. There is something quite refined about this tradition. Cloth runs the length of most tasteful tables, but it can be replaced easily with glorious branches of any variety. Spice up your table by designing your own natural runner. Branches are always in season and never hard to find. These white birch limbs are exceptionally elegant and fit right in with the delicate linens to form a cozy setting. Here is an outstanding opportunity to blend natural colors and textures and design a unique dining experience. Set for a memorable evening of good food and fellowship, the casual charm of this creative table is simply irresistible.

PURE ARTISTRY

After heavy rains or strong winds, you might be lucky enough to come across a particularly beautiful branch that has fallen from a tree. Why not incorporate it into your decorating scheme, allowing its natural beauty to be the main attraction?

Our designer found these dogwood branches in her own front yard. Inspired by their tripod design, she created a pair of freestanding sculptures. She leveled the base of the branches to sit flat on the floor. Insects had eaten some of the branch bark, leaving a decorative pattern in their wake. She removed parts of the remaining bark to expose more of the design. When making your own tripod branches, you can leave them in their natural state or rub them with a coat of linseed oil for a darker, more polished finish.

NATURE'S CULTURE

Many tropical houseplants boast exotic leaf designs. Their appeal comes from bold colors, unusual silhouettes, and strong patterns. Can you see the resemblance between this leaf and an African mask? By displaying the leaf and the mask together, you open a visual dialogue between nature and culture.

This striking leaf came from the *Alocasia amazonica*, more commonly known as the African mask, elephant's ear, kris plant, or green velvet plant. Encountering this plant, it's plain to see how it gained such fanciful common names. Its spectacular scalloped foliage and moderate maintenance requirements make the African mask a favorite with indoor jungle gardeners. The African mask is easy to grow, provided you keep it in a warm room with high humidity and away from direct sun. When trimming a single stem for presentation, cut close to the base of the plant. To extend the life of the leaf, you can insert the end of the stem into a floral tube filled with water.

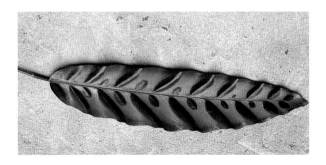

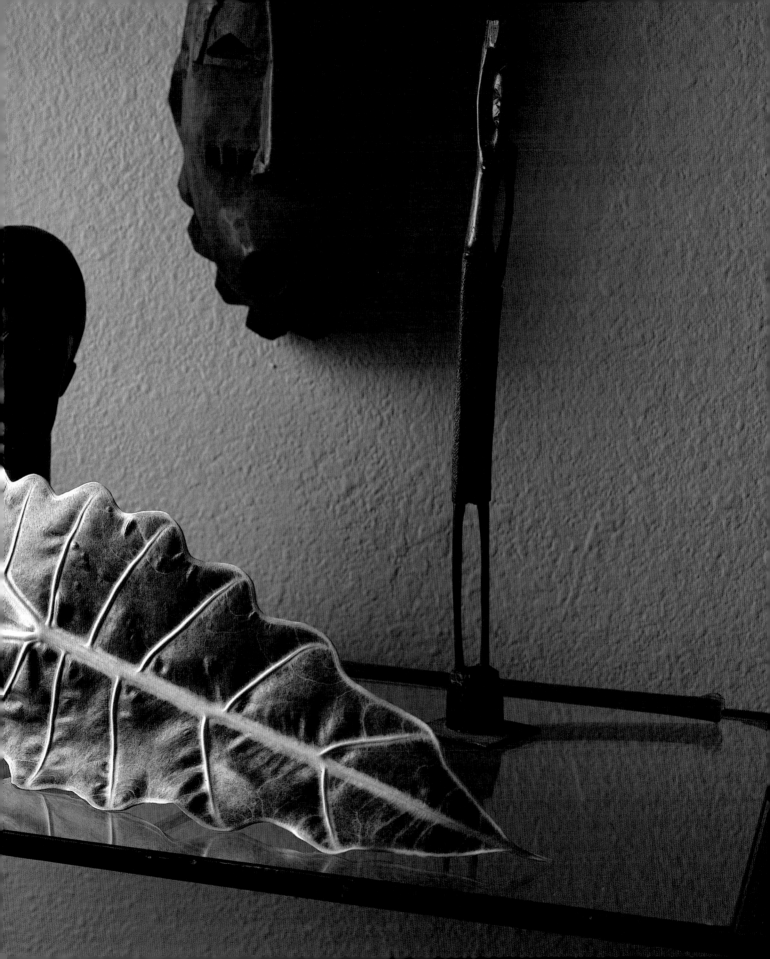

BACK PORCH
NIRVANA

As you decorate with nature, you'll enjoy tinkering with the placement of many different types of objects until you create a satisfying design. This tranquil tableau provides the perfect backdrop for you to linger over breakfast, read a good book, or just sit peacefully to absorb the atmosphere. The quiet round river rocks and lush succulent leaves counterbalance the bold, colorful curtain. The blue-green foliage harmonizes with the cool gray tones of their pots and the large stones. Notice that two pots have plants with leaves that reach upwards, while two are trailing varieties. The distressed surface of the painted wood cabinet provides an interesting contrast to the rocks.

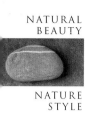

LEAF SCROLL
BOATS

Fireplace hearths don't have to be dreary. Counter sooty darkness with a quick arrangement of twigs, leaves, and candles; then sit back and enjoy the way the flickering light shows off nature's simple beauty.

To create the leaf installation, select leaves from the same species of plant. It's best to use leaves that are long, narrow, and thin. (The variegated varieties are particularly nice.) Choose one leaf for the boat, and set it aside. Beginning at the stem end, roll one leaf into a loose tube. Once you reach the top of the pointed end, apply a bit of candle wax or glue stick to its underside, and press down. Repeat this process until you have enough leaf spirals to fill your boat. Arrange the spirals vertically, horizontally, or a combination of both, maintaining an Asian-inspired style. Once the leaf boat begins to fade, you can ceremoniously launch it into the fire.

T W I G   B A S K E T

Everywhere you go, keep an eye out for interesting decorating materials. Sometimes they'll turn up in the most unusual places. It's especially exciting to realize a totally new use for an object other than its intended function. Once you stretch your imagination this way, you'll find raw materials all around.

This accordion-style twig basket was sold as an outdoor gardening supply. Its real use is to surround plants and flowers, protecting them as they grow. (To picture this, reverse the top and bottom of the basket.) Our designers were enchanted by the shape and movement of the object as well as its being formed from natural materials. They immediately knew it had potential to be transformed into an indoor objet d'art.

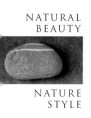
SPIRITUAL
HARMONY

Leaves, twigs, and stones blend with the textured walls, distressed furniture, architectural salvage, and other components of today's easygoing interiors. This design unites the diverse elements of stone, ceramics, metal, wood, glass, and fabric. Their only common trait is a feeling of time-honored and carefree elegance.

FIREPLACE SPACE

We've all developed specific rituals to mark the transition of the seasons. Here is a new and popular decorating practice you'll want to add to your annual schedule.

After the glowing embers of your last winter fire die, transform the empty space into a contemporary design niche. The typical recessed fireplace provides an attractive staging area for all kinds of natural arrangements. Use branches, twigs, leaves, stones, or any combination of materials to create your design.

PRINCESS HATIM & THE ALMOND TREE

Almond trees have been cultivated in Morocco for centuries. These beautiful trees line many of the roads, and every spring the Trafout Festival celebrates the short-lived blossoms of these trees. This is a tale told in Morocco about the almond tree:

Once there was a princess named Hatim, whom Allah had blessed with a kind and generous soul. When anyone asked her for food or money, Princess Hatim would oblige them. She could not refuse someone in need, and her fortune was soon exhausted and her possessions gone. But still the hungry and poor came to her—so Princess Hatim stole from the Royal Treasury. Before long, Princess Hatim came forward and admitted her guilt. Furious, her father offered her a choice: be exiled in disgrace or die.

Without a moment's hesitation, Princess Hatim chose to die. She told her father that exile was the worse fate, because she would see the people's suffering but be unable to alleviate it.

On the morning that Princess Hatim was to be executed, Allah turned her into an almond tree, to forever provide food and comfort to the people of Morocco. Her nuts and oil feed the hungry, and her beautiful flowers console the heavy-hearted.

STUDIED STONES

Stones create a majestic yet down-to-earth feel in your home that is always in fashion. This attractive bowl presentation may be the epitome of natural style. Much of its beauty comes from simplicity.

Gather a group of appealing stones and set them before you. Focus on each individual stone, contemplating its unique traits, and then mindfully reduce your selections to the most outstanding stones. Position them in a plain bowl. Adjust their relationships and angles until you're satisfied that the stones are showing all their best sides, and then leave them alone. Place the bowl in a busy but comfortable location in your home. The goal is for you to evaluate the composition both through fleeting glances and prolonged contemplation over an extended period of time. After living with the untouched arrangement, you'll feel a deeper connection to its elements and be able to regard the composition as a whole.

Mary Ellen Long.
Rock Spiral, 1991.
Outdoor installation.
Photo by artist.

FRESH POCKETS

Send a splendid spring greeting to everyone at your table with these stylish pastel slipcovers. Individual arrangements of fresh-cut leaves and berries are tucked gracefully into a rear pocket. The light cotton is as fresh as a flower, and sewing it into simple slipcovers is a breeze. Those seasoned folding chairs you thought were past their prime suddenly take on new life when dressed for dinner. Contrasting tones of dark rustic wood furniture, pale fabrics, and vibrant leaves combine to create a memorable environment.

Fresh filler for the slipcover pockets can be assembled in a flash. Snip whatever is healthy and growing in your yard, fashion an arrangement, and then fit it into a floral tube to keep it thriving. Tuck one or more tubes into each pocket, adding additional embellishments if you desire. Ambitious decorators can adapt this idea to fit any time of year and color scheme. Heavier fabrics and evergreen or dried foliage would be delightful for winter.

SEASON'S CYCLE

As the dark days of winter come to a close, some of the earliest, most welcome signs of spring are budding willow trees and other blossoming branches. There are several ways to prolong the enjoyment of this natural phenomenon indoors.

One option is to force the stems to bloom indoors. Forcing blooms is a traditional way to enjoy the spring show of many plant species. Cut the branches just when their buds are starting to swell, and bring them indoors. Use a utility knife to shave about 2 inches (5 cm) of bark off the twig above where it was cut. To help the branch absorb water, slightly crush the shaved area. Fill a deep vase with room-temperature water, arrange the branches in the container, and then place it in full sun. The buds will bloom approximately two to four weeks after they are brought inside.

The graceful swaying limbs of large willow trees are a familiar sight. Decorative pussy willows, however, come from smaller trees with colorful stems and leaves, and exquisite catkins, the renowned fuzzy buds. Pussy willow catkins come in a delightful assortment of colors, ranging from silver gray to pale pink to jet black.

Pussy willows can be forced to bloom or preserved as tiny buds. Just snip the pussy willow twigs, mist them with hair spray, and then bring them into your home. Whether you selected twigs with tight buds or ones more fully open, the catkins will remain at that stage forever. This simple technique prepares the pussy willows for any dried-flower arrangement you choose to create.

PUSSY WILLOWS

Here are some choice willow varieties that produce attractive catkins:

Florist's pussy willow (Salix caprea) has large gray catkins that steadily become yellow as they mature. This tree is also commonly called the French, goat, or pink willow.

Japanese pussy willow (S. chaenomeloides) is a fantastic variety for winter cutting. Its large catkins can grow up to 2½ inches (6.4 cm) long. Japanese pussy willows are silvery gray but assume a pink appearance with age. In winter, the bare mahogany red stems of the Japanese pussy willow are glorious. This tree is also commonly called the quince-leafed pussy willow.

Corkscrew willows (S. matsudana "Tortuosa") are tailor-made for interior design as their limbs and branches twist and turn, and their catkins are pronounced. This tree is also known as the dragon's claw willow.

Fantail willows (S. udensis "Sekka") have distinctive twisted stems with wide flat ends. Their small, silvery catkins are abundant and turn soft yellow as they mature.

Black pussy willows (S. gracilistyla melanostachys) may be the most dramatic-looking pussy willow. The anthers on the black catkins slowly turn yellow, providing a spectacle that lasts for weeks. Because of their growing formation, black pussy willows don't have long simple stems like most pussy willows. You'll only have about 8-inch (20.3 cm) stems to work with in your arrangements, so small vases are recommended.

MORE TO MAKE WITH STONES

There are endless opportunities to decorate with stones. Our fascination with stones generated more projects and ideas than could be contained in this book. Here are a few we highly recommend.

STREAMING CENTERPIECE

Conversation will flow like a stream across this arrangement. Use smooth stones—polished, if you wish—to create this serene tableau. Add some candles for soft lighting, perhaps. If you're fortunate enough to have a brook on your property, you'll have ready access to the perfect materials for this natural table runner.

SLATE SUSHI PLATTER

The Zen nature of this material perfectly complements the food that is served upon it. Slate is durable and won't stain; chill the platter before serving, to keep the sushi cool and fresh. Though slate is commonly thought of as black or gray, it's actually found in nature in a variety of hues and is commercially available in a multitude of colors, so you'll be able to find a piece that suits your mood.

WRAPPED STONES

Make holiday decorating beautifully simple when you tie a graceful bow around smooth stones. Red satin is stunning, but you could also choose velvet, raffia, or even metallics. Consider the possibilities of wire, too, with beads intertwined for sparkle. However, let your bow material enhance the shape and character of the stones, not surpass it.

TRANQUIL CAIRN

Cairns have been used since ancient times to serve as memorials or markers. Some cultures constructed them in the form of humans, built to stand for eternity. Assemble your cairn in a cherished spot in your home, letting it mark a place of tranquility or beauty. Choose smooth or rough stones (either could be appropriate), and take time to enjoy the meditative building process.

EXTRA IDEAS

- For a tasteful table accent, sandwich place cards between two small stones.
- Want a super soap dish? Line a little tray with pebbles.
- Any weighty stone can be a doorstop or a paperweight. (Affix felt pads to the bottom to protect your floors and tables.)
- Create unique drawer and cabinet pulls out of round stones.
- Add a stone to the end of your fan chain.
- If you enjoy aromatherapy, try placing a few drops of essential oil on top of porous stones.
- Decorate a thumbtack with a pebble.
- Transform a beautiful piece of slate into a trivet or cheese tray.
- Stones trap both heat and cold. Place warmed stones at the bottom of a bread basket and chilled stones in a wine bucket.

EARLY BLOOMERS

Flowering twigs loosen a cold winter's grip by brightening rooms with cheerful color. Eager gardeners can get a jump on the season by forcing spring-flowering trees and shrubs to bloom indoors. Outdoors, these blossoming branches can be overpowered by spring's profusion of magnificent flowers. Forced to bloom inside the house, these familiar twigs will seem positively exotic. Crabapple, flowering quince, forsythia, magnolia, redbud, serviceberry, and some fruit trees can be forced to flower indoors.

In order for the twigs to bloom, you'll need to replicate early spring-like weather conditions inside your home. Most importantly, the twigs require adequate moisture and humidity. During the day, position the twigs in a bright but not overly sunny place, and then move them to a cool location at night. Always have fresh water for your twigs, and recut their stems as needed. Keep a close eye on the buds so you can create your arrangement just prior to their bursting; this not only prevents flower damage, but lets you enjoy watching and smelling the flowers as they come into their full glory. Your new blooms will last as long indoors as they do outside.

Gina Telcocci.
Willow Whisper, 1997.
Willow and wire.
Photo by artist.

PODS OF GOLD

Identifying and intensifying the artistic traits of your natural materials will help you create more impressive arrangements. Placing a *Lunaria* twig (commonly known as the money plant, gypsy dollar, or silver dollar) into a glass vessel isn't difficult, but you must have the courage to let the twig stand on its own.

When I evaluate the beauty of the Lunaria stem, three distinguishing features come to mind: their oval seed pods hanging from slender stems with the nimbleness of an Alexander Calder mobile; the translucence of their paper-thin pods, which occasionally reveal the contour of the dark seeds held within; and the striking color combination of rich burgundy and green. When you find just the right design element, the "less is more" principle is both accurate and reliable.

LIVELY IVY

Picture any ivy-covered structure in your mind. Whether it's a castle or a college, chances are a substantial sprawl of ivy evokes an image of dignity and durability. Ivy-growers might conjure up another picture: fast-growing and unruly ivy taking over everything! Most ivy growers have such an abundance of the vine that they're ecstatic to share. When you plan to decorate with ivy, alert your friends and neighbors, and you're sure to receive an ample supply.

An ivy vine looks magnificent coiled around a pillar candle inside a hurricane lamp. This quick-and-easy arrangement is a real eye-catcher, naturalizing the industrial appearance of glass and metal. Since ivy vines are flexible, you can hang them like garlands or streamers for unique party decorations. Once the vines are cut, their leaves will continue to thrive for several days.

POETIC PAIR

When we look to nature for our design inspiration, we're consulting the finest source. Noticing what materials exist together outdoors will help you make inspired choices for your indoor arrangements that appear incredibly spontaneous. Because these leaves and stones are neighbors in the wild, they also make a perfectly natural-looking couple indoors

To create a similar centerpiece, artfully arrange a few stones in a shallow bowl, add water, and then add two or three water plants. The leaves of the water plants have a waxy appearance that intensifies when displayed against pitted and sedate gray river rocks. Because the rocks are partially submerged, you'll enjoy both their wet and dry looks.

WARDING STONES

People throughout Asia have used special stones to protect their houses and families from evil for more than a thousand years.

Most of these "warding" stones have the words Shi Gandang on their surface. Shi Gandang means "stone that dares to undertake formidable tasks in the face of enemies." Placed in front of a home's main gate, or at any door that opens onto the street, warding stones keep evil spirits and negative energies at bay.

The Chinese village of Uan-Lim has a warding stone that protects the entire town. According to legend, the village's crops failed year after year, leaving the villagers in peril for the winter. Their last seeds were planted with heavy hearts.

That night, a villager dreamt of a man who told him the crops failed because evil spirits ate them. To drive out the spirits, the man said, dig on the left side of the tree in the center of town.

In the morning, the villager and his neighbors dug until they uncovered a large, cylindrical rock. They pulled it out of the ground and built a temple around it. The next morning, every single seed had sprouted. Villagers offered the rock incense and worshipped it. The crops continued to grow, and produced enough food to feed the entire village through the winter.

45

CLOAKED ROSES

A single white rose wrapped in one luscious green leaf brings nature's quiet sophistication to your table. Any doubts you may have about your floral arranging skills will quickly be dispelled once you create this easy arrangement.

To assemble this design, lay one leaf on your work surface, and then place a rose on top. Position the blossom about ¼ inch (6 mm) below the top of the leaf. Snip the stem of the rose at an angle (under cold water if possible) so it fits just below the leaf's bottom edge. Roll the leaf around the rose, and place the bundle in a shallow clear cordial glass to hold it tight. Add about 1 inch (2.5 cm) of cold water to the bottom of the glass so the rose and leaf will thrive.

BALANCING ACT

When you see shiny glass marbles at the bottom of a vase, they are being used as decorative filler to help keep the flower stems in place. Naturally waterproof and heavy, stones are an equally efficient stabilizer. Because they occur together in the landscape, stones and flowers are perfect companions for forming simple and earthy arrangements without the dirt.

Using vase filler lets you design gorgeous arrangements in a wider variety of containers. Even if you have only a few blossoms to work with, you can tie them together with coarse twine, stand them upright in the center of the vase, and then anchor them with stones. This method is a welcome solution for the challenge of designing in wide-mouth containers.

FORM & FUNCTION

NATURAL ACCENTS CAN WARM UP YOUR HOME, AND BE USEFUL, AS THIS CHAPTER DEMONSTRATES SO BEAUTIFULLY. FROM BIRCH DRESSER PULLS TO A PRINTED LEAF CUSHION, THESE IMAGINATIVE AND PRACTICAL PROJECTS HAVE PLENTY OF ENVIRONMENTAL APPEAL. TO MAKE YOUR DINING EXPERIENCE POSITIVELY ORGANIC, WE'VE ALSO INCLUDED SCRUMPTIOUS IDEAS FOR DECORATING TABLES WITH NATURAL STYLE.

MEDITATION
GARDEN

Z en rock gardening is a peaceful practice. The Japanese developed dry gardens to encourage meditation on the principles of Zen philosophy. The rock garden is a minimalist landscape where large rocks represent mountains, and "islands" appear within a "sea" of crushed stone. The stones are meticulously raked into symbolic and serene patterns.

It's possible to reinterpret the rock garden on a much smaller scale, thus allowing you to embark on a contemplative practice and raking ritual in the comfort of your home. Define the boundaries of your garden with the interior edges of a black lacquer tray. Cover the bottom of the tray with soft sand. (In this miniature version, sand replaces the customary crushed stone.) Select two or more stones that suggest diminutive mountains or island forms, and place them in the sand. Slowly drag your rake through the sand to create formal patterns without beginning or end. Buddhists believe that when regularly and mindfully practiced, Zen rock gardening eases stress and opens the pathway to a clearer head and more caring heart.

PULLING IT TOGETHER

In less than a day, you can give a plain chest of drawers an incredible makeover using natural materials. Twigs make sensible and stylish drawer pulls, and a simple decoupaged collage of pretty papers heightens the overall effect.

Plant materials—leaves and twigs—are the building blocks of paper. Some papers feature *inclusions*, or identifiable leaves, petals, and strands. These sheets are sold in most craft and art supply stores. Each piece of paper is unique. You'll need several sheets of different papers to create this project.

PREPARING THE CHEST OF DRAWERS

Remove all hardware from the drawer fronts, and then, if desired, paint or stain the wood.

PIECING THE PAPER

Prepare the collage by tearing simple geometric shapes of paper for each drawer. To create the background motif, tear a single rectangle of paper that is slightly smaller than the drawer face. Tear several more shapes, such as squares, triangles, and rectangles, from different sheets of paper. Play with differ-

ent arrangements of the paper shapes on top of the background rectangle. When you're satisfied with one arrangement, set it aside. Create additional paper collages for each drawer.

DECOUPAGING THE DRAWERS

Adhere the papers to the drawers with decoupage medium, following the manufacturer's instructions. Apply the background paper first, then the smaller shapes. Allow each layer to dry as directed. Seal the completed drawer front with decoupage medium or clear varnish.

FORMING & ATTACHING THE TWIG HANDLES

Look at the back sides of the drawer fronts, and find the holes drilled for the original hardware. Use an awl or other sharp pointed tool to poke through the paper layers on each drawer. Measure between the holes, and then cut your twigs somewhat longer than this distance. Attach the twigs to the front of the drawers with wood screws placed through the holes from the back.

ENHANCING YOUR VIEW

Gorgeous colors and textures are just the right pick-me-up for this plain-colored curtain. A carefree grouping of leaves, pinecones, nuts, and pods is the focal point for this most unusual tie-back. These natural elements attach to flexible vines that can be bent with ease into sensational ribbon-like spirals.

To create this curtain trim, start by collecting fresh vines in the wild, or purchasing vines from craft supply stores. Decorate the vine with patches of green moss for extra color and texture. Use a clear-drying all-purpose craft glue to adhere the moss to the vine, and let dry. Wrap the vine around your curtain to determine the length you need for the tie-back. Shape the excess vine into the pattern of your choice. Remove the vine from the curtain, and then embellish the end as desired, using floral wire to connect the natural materials. This particular design is unusual because it features the backs of leaves, highlighting their intricate ribbed structure.

RAISE THE BAR

This imaginative display is simple to fashion and makes the most of natural light to illuminate collected treasures. Choose a handsome and sturdy twig for the bar. Raised knobs on the twig are attractive and help keep loosely tied ornament hangers in their place. To suspend the twig, wrap each end with twine, and then make a secure knot. (This design uses two strands of different colors of twine on each side of the bar.) Tie the opposite ends of the twine around an existing curtain rod or two nails. Adjust the length of the hanging twine as needed until the bar is level. Select the decorative elements you wish to use, and string them with coarse natural fiber such as twine, raffia, hemp, or jute. The ornaments suspended from this bar come mostly from organic sources and feature a similar palette. Use wire to hang heavier elements, such as the clear glass candleholder. Vary the lengths and spacing of the lines according to the object being hung and your artistic taste.

SPEAKING
VOLUMES

Sometimes the simplest ideas are the best, such as stationing one or more stones on your bookshelf to prop up your library. Stones are heavy and handy, of course, but they're more than merely functional. Used as bookends, stones suggest fortitude and longevity. Stone book-ends make excellent gifts that everyone can enjoy. Outside the home, they can be a welcome and beautiful addition to offices, waiting rooms, and retail displays.

A quick trip to any masonry yard yields extensive choices of flat-edge stones, although uncut varieties will also work. If you'd like retain the look of wet stone, you can shine your bookends with jeweler's polish or vegetable oil. Many other natural materials make extraordinary bookends. Depending on your taste and the style of your home, you can experi-ment with sandstone, agate, geode, crystal, jasper, calcite, and even petrified wood.

MATO TIPI

A solitary rock juts over 1,200 feet (366 m) above the surrounding flat landscape in northeastern Wyoming. Early explorers named the imposing monolith Devil's Tower. But various Native American cultures had other names for it, including Mato Tipi, *the bear lodge.* Several peoples

have stories about its formation; here is a variation of the Kiowa version:

Seven little girls were playing on the outskirts of their village when a hungry bear chased them away from their home. They ran and ran—each step taking them farther from safety.

Finally, they collapsed on a low rock ledge and prayed that the rock would save them from the approaching bear. With a low rum-ble, the ledge began to

rise. It rose higher and higher, lifting the girls beyond the bear's reach. But the bear did not give up; she dug her long, sharp claws into the sides of the rock and began to climb, but each time the bear slid to the ground, furrowing deep gashes in the rock's surface. Finally, the bear's claws were worn away.

The rock, however, had risen until it touched the sky, and the girls were turned into stars. Today, this cluster is known as the Pleiades, the Seven Sisters.

CUSHIONS WITH CHARACTER

Creating unique pillows is one of the simplest decorating projects you can undertake to personalize your home. The fabric design for this elegant cushion was taken directly from nature. Modern fabric paints and dyes can be easily applied in many different ways to alter textiles. Rather than relying on the prints and colors available at your local retailer, you can design your own fabrics.

The leaf image on this cushion was created using a simple form of relief printmaking. To make it yourself, you'll need a large deep-veined leaf, such as one from a tropical houseplant. You'll also need to gather a paintbrush, fabric paint, paper towels, and a small sponge roller. Iron your cushion fabric, and then position it right side up on a sturdy, level work surface. Carefully brush the fabric paint onto the side of the leaf with the raised veins. Lay the leaf onto the fabric with the painted side down, placing paper towels or a thin cloth on top. Use the sponge roller to transfer the fabric paint from the leaf to the cloth. Gently lift the towel and leaf off the fabric to unveil your print. Allow the paint to dry, according to the manufacturer's instructions. With its one-of-a-kind natural design, your new fabric is now ready to be sewn into a beautiful cushion.

OUT OF THE ORDINARY CANDLEHOLDERS

Transforming an everyday stone into an exceptionally attractive candleholder is essentially effortless. Stability and versatility make stone candleholders ideal accessories for outdoor decorating, where they'll faithfully weather the elements.

AROMATIC HERB & WIRE WRAP

To create the project shown below, first select a large flat stone. (Flat stones provide a balanced base and a level decorating surface.) The stone's diameter should be larger than the tea light candle you intend to use. Wrap the stone with 16-gauge wire, making several full rotations in a single direction. If desired, twist the wire, and then work in the perpendicular

direction. Center one tea light candle on the top of the stone. Circle the candle with another length of wire to form a secure nest. Bend the wire in an arbitrary fashion for artistic flair. Bond the bottom of the candle to the top of the stone with candle wax or other suitable adhesive. For the finishing touch, slide sprigs of lavender between the wires. Freshly picked leaves, fuzzy and gray-green, have an enchanting scent.

VINE & GARLAND TRIM

Large stones also make striking candleholders for oversize votives and short pillars. Use the color, shape, and texture of the stone for inspiration when selecting the candle and embellishments. Here are two lovely design options that use natural materials to disguise the seam between the candle and the stone. Below is a miniature wreath made from fresh leaves (see page 118 for instructions), and on the left is a simple vine loop with a wrapped wire accent. Both these projects are amazing because they are simple to make, and you probably already have the materials on hand. They also complement all sorts of interiors, from the sleekest contemporary loft to the most rustic country cabin.

STONE & CANDLE TABLEAU

Candles have been "must haves" for the home for years. They're inherently romantic, and often used in aromatherapy and feng shui. Strategically placed near check-outs in many home accessory stores, candles are an impulse purchase for grown-ups—the decora-

tor's candy bar. As shown on the right, displaying candles in a variety of heights, widths, colors, and fragrances with a stone collection paints a very artistic picture. Count yourself particularly lucky if you've found stones with naturally occurring holes.

A small tin of candle adhesive is a great product to keep around the house. It only takes a tiny pinch of the adhesive to firmly bond a candle to its base. Most adhesives work best when they're "warmed up," or briefly rubbed between your index finger and thumb prior to use. If you're using a stone that doesn't have a flat surface on which to adhere your candle, you may want to shave the candle's base with an ordinary table knife to make it fit. Remove the wax in small increments, slowly shaping the candle to the contour of your stone.

COAT TREE

Remember staring at cloud forms, and noticing that their shapes suggested other things? One look at this twig, and the idea to create a coat rack instantly sprang to the designer's imagination. However, she didn't rush into adapting the twig to suit her needs. The twig lived on her porch for some time. This led the designer to a fuller appreciation of the twig's shape and thereby to a more sensitive final design.

Make a pencil sketch of your twig on a piece of paper. Use its form to inspire a drawing for the twig base. Think of function and flow as you consider different options. Once you've created an agreeable base, contact a local metal artisan to bring your idea to life.

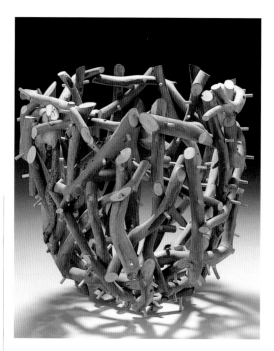

Gyöngy Laky.
Limbs and Fingers, 2001.
Eucalyptus prunings and
wooden dowels.
Photo by M. Lee Fatherree.

MATCHING WITS

You'll love testing your backgammon skill on this back-to-basics game board. Its cool palette is relaxing, allowing you to focus on your strategy.

PREPARING THE WOOD

You'll need two equal-size rectangles of plywood to make the game board. Create two holes in each board to accommodate the ribbon strap. Paint both sides of the plywood solid white, and let dry.

PAINTING THE POINTS

Add the 24 narrow triangles, called *points*, in charcoal and slate acrylic paints. This would be a great opportunity to create linoleum or sponge stamps to standardize the design of your points. Alternate colors, as you paint or stamp four quadrants of six triangles each. (Each quadrant is the player's home or outer board. They are separated from each other by a space down the center of the board called the *bar*.) Once your paint dries, seal it with a thin, even coat of clear spray varnish in a matte finish.

WEAVING THE RIBBON

Feed a sturdy grosgrain ribbon up through one hole in one side of the board, then down through the hole on the facing board. Pull the ribbon so it's even on both sides of the board. Repeat this for the second set of holes.

PLAY ON!

Each player will need 15 playing pieces, or *checkers*, of one color. Small smooth river stones, as soothing to the eye as they are to the touch, make ideal checkers. Choose contrasting colored stones, such as gray and white, to clarify play. Once you've played your last game of the day, just tie the ribbons in loose bows to close the board. Store your checkers in a drawstring canvas bag until you're in the mood for a rematch.

TIMBER LAMP

You can make this elegant yet rustic-looking lamp with an assortment of driftwood pieces. All you need are simple lamp-making materials, a drill, a cache of driftwood, and the desire to create.

BEFORE YOU BEGIN

You can purchase a lamp base, or craft one from an 8 x 8-inch (20.3 x 20.3 cm) piece of wood. Weathered wood is a great match for the driftwood, but any wood base will do. You'll need a basic lamp kit which includes a threaded brass rod. Lamp kits are sold at home improvement stores. They require a minimal amount of wiring, instructions for which are explained on the kit. If electrical wiring gives you the shivers, find a lamp shop in your area to do the wiring for you. Wait to select a lamp shade until after you have wired the lamp.

BUILDING THE LAMP

Begin by attaching the threaded brass rod to your lamp base. Select a drill bit that is slightly larger than the diameter of the threaded rod. Place a piece of driftwood on a piece of scrapwood, and then drill a hole completely through the center of the driftwood. Repeat this process for each driftwood piece. Next, slip the driftwood pieces onto the rod, and play with their placement before you wire the lamp. (Once the lamp is wired, you won't be able to move them around.) Leave about 1 inch (2.5 cm) of the top of the brass rod exposed so you can later attach the harp and socket. Finally, wire the lamp following the manufacturer's instructions, or take it to a lamp shop.

FINISHING TOUCHES

Once you purchase a shade, you can embellish it if desired. A quick-and-easy method is to hot glue small pebbles or scraps of driftwood around the top and base of the shade. If you're lucky enough to find beach pebbles with naturally occurring holes, thread them onto coarse twine and tie them to the shade.

COASTAL MOBILE

Creating a mobile is a balancing act: adding a little here and a little there until it pleases your eye and hangs well. The simple charm of this mobile comes from its casual construction. Lengths of easy-to-cut and twist wire are threaded through holes or wound around natural objects. No rocket science here—just determine if you need a larger shell on this side or three small rocks on that side, and go with the flow.

PREPARING THE MATERIALS

Select your materials with an eye toward their future use. Ideally, your shells and stones should have holes. It's possible to drill through stone, but it's not an simple task. Driftwood pieces can be easily drilled if needed, but naturally occurring holes are preferable.

CREATING THE HANGING STRUCTURE

Select two long pieces of wood. Drill a hole in the center and at each end of both pieces. Cut a length of 22-gauge wire, thread it through both center holes, and wind it around several times to loosely join the wood. Create a hanging wire, and attach it to the crossed wood pieces.

HANGING THE ORNAMENTS

Wrap one end of a generous length of wire (far more than you think you'll need) around a stone, and secure it by twisting the wire's end. Thread shells, stones, or small pieces of driftwood onto the wire. Twist the wire to secure the objects. When you're pleased with the length, attach it to the cross pieces through the central holes.

BALANCING THE MOBILE

Now, for the balancing act. Follow the process in the previous step to create more decorated wire lengths. If you're feeling bold, you can slip small driftwood pieces onto the wire, treating them as mini-hanging structures, just like the large crosspiece. Attach wire to the ends of each crosspiece, balancing it with shells and stones. You may find that you need to add or subtract a piece as you go.

MORE TO MAKE WITH TWIGS

Add the simple designs below to the twig ideas and projects in this book, and you're sure to have plenty to kindle your imagination. Inspired by little twigs, our designer produced a lot of big ideas we hope you'll enjoy.

ALPHABET TWIGS

What fun you can have with these fanciful letters…tie a balloon around your child's initial for a special greeting, or insert flowers through the letters when you create a romantic message for a loved one. Take that special someone on a walk as you look for twigs that can be fashioned into the alphabet—and take along a bottle of wine, perhaps?

EMBELLISHED FRAME

Twigs accentuate these rustic frames; is there any better way to display cherished photos in your cabin or hideaway? You can, of course, use any color to crackle-paint the frame, and add twigs as you wish for decoration. Maybe you would prefer to embellish the corners of the frame, rather than the sides? There is ample opportunity for creative interpretation with this project.

FLOWERPOT POWER

A simple idea can yield a number of possibilities, like these terra-cotta flowerpots artfully arrayed with twigs. Depending upon the shape of the pot you choose, many options are available; how about twining a flexible vine around a vase? Consider twigs from a species of tree with showy bark to add some excitement. Think of your flowerpot as a blank canvas, and then release your imagination.

BRANCH HANGERS

Put these delightful hangers on center stage—don't hide them in your closet! Hang them on a wall to exhibit a colorful item of ethnic clothing; use several in a group to display collections of scarves or belts; or simply have tomorrow's wardrobe at your fingertips when the alarm clock rings. A delicate garment will certainly add some romance to these utilitarian creations.

CHOPSTICK REST

Form meets function here as nature designs these twigs to hold chopsticks. Consider using pieces from assorted trees to provide contrast in color and in the texture of bark; enhance the individuality of these rests by giving each diner chopsticks of a different design and plates that are unique. Translate this idea to your kitchen, and use a twig to rest a spoon or ladle while you cook.

EXTRA IDEAS

- *Construct a simple decorative twig ladder.*
- *Set your soap sailing in the bathtub atop a twig raft.*
- *Make candy apples even better with natural twig handles.*

BOXED STONES

While driving past the local masonry yard, our designer caught sight of stones neatly stacked in heavy wire fencing. This chance encounter was his inspiration. Boxing stones in wire mesh is a sleek and orderly way to display your collection. Metal and stone complement each other with a distinctly modern flair.

FINDING YOUR MATERIAL

The boxes are made from hardware cloth, a stiff wire net that you'll find in the fencing or gardening section of home improvement centers. The ¼- or ½-inch (6 mm and 1.3 cm) grids are easiest to work with and suit most stones.

MAKING THE PATTERN

Examine your stone or stones to determine the size of the box you wish to make. Place the stones on a sheet of paper, stacking them as needed. Sketch a square or rectangle around the stones onto a sheet of lightweight cardboard, and then use a ruler and pencil to create a more precise shape. Cut out the drawing to make the pattern for one side of the box.

PREPARING THE HARDWARE CLOTH

Unroll the hardware cloth, and flatten it with your hands. Place the pattern on the cloth; picture an area that is four patterns high and three patterns wide; then use wire snips to cut off enough cloth to accommodate all sides of the box.

MARKING THE BOX PATTERN

Use the method that follows to form the full pattern on the hardware cloth. The complete pattern is shaped like a cross. Position the paper pattern in the center of the cloth. (This paper is only a guide. If the edges of the pattern do not precisely match the lines of the wire grid, enlarge the pattern to fit on the grid.) Use a pen to mark the pattern shape on the grid, and then remove the paper. Mark the same shape on each adjacent side of the first marked shape. To be precise, count the squares of the grid to mark equal shapes. To complete marking the pattern, add another pattern shape adjacent to any of the preciously marked pattern shapes.

CUTTING & BENDING THE HARDWARE CLOTH

Use wire snips to cut out the marked pattern. Snip closely along the edges where wires cross. Remove the small bumps on the edges of the wire with a flat or half-round file. Using a scrap of 2 x 4 (5 x 10.2 cm) lumber as an edge, you're going to "upset" the sides of the box. Gently bend up the box, one side at time, making a bend in the last side or top.

SEWING THE SIDES

Cut a length of 22- or 24-gauge steel wire that is twice as long as the height of the box sides. Working from the bottom of the box, join two sides together, twisting ½ inch (1.3 cm) of the end of the wire back onto the longer length. Use pliers to securely twist the wire. Use the wire like thread to whipstitch the side of the box. Make a stitch in every grid square. Whipstitch to the top of the joined sides, leaving the end of the wire free. Repeat this process to join the remaining box sides.

FINISHING THE BOX

Place your stones in the box, and fold over the mesh top. Use the free ends of the wires to whipstitch the lid closed. Wrap the wire tightly at the end, and then snip off any excess.

SETTING YOUR TABLECLOTH

Dining al fresco is a delight, but sudden winds can upset your carefully arranged table. Here's a clever and stylish solution that will naturally anchor your linens even after the dishes are cleared.

Find four flat stones of ample weight and width. Each stone should be about 2 to 3 inches (5 to 7.6 cm) high and 5 inches (12.7 cm) in diameter. For each stone, cut a long piece of coarse twine. Tightly wrap one end of the twine around one corner of the tablecloth, making two or three rotations. (Leave a decorative tail of twine before beginning the wrap.) Secure the twine to the cloth with a strong knot, and let the length of excess twine fall naturally to the floor. Position one rock on the ground, and bind it with the twine. Criss-cross the twine around and under the stone as if you were adding ribbon to a gift package. Tie off the second end of the twine, leaving another decorative tail. Remove any slack in the twine by angling the rock away from the cloth. Repeat this process on all four corners.

THE WEIGHT OF THE MATTER

Single stones make attractive napkin weights. Simply place one stone on top of each piece of folded cloth, and voila—a super stylish setting.

NATURE IN PRINT

Get in the spirit of spring by adorning a set of table linens with vivid foliage prints. Used indoors or out, these lively linens are a fantastic reminder of nature's energy and continuous renewal. This one-of-a-kind textile design isn't found in stores, and no two efforts will ever produce the same results. One simple printmaking technique is all that is required to make this project, so roll up your sleeves and get started.

GATHERING THE MATERIALS

To create the print, you'll need a plain, light-colored tablecloth and four or more fresh twigs from plants or trees. Each twig should be fairly small, with about four to five thickly veined leaves attached. Also have on hand a paintbrush, fabric paints in a variety of invigorating greens, paper towels, and a small sponge roller.

PRINTING THE CLOTH

Iron the tablecloth if needed, and then lay it flat on a sturdy, level work surface. (If you're working in a small space, you can print the cloth in sections. Each one will need to dry completely before you print another area.) Select one color of fabric paint to use first. Carefully brush a thin layer of the paint onto the underside of the leaves and stems of one twig. Gently place the twig onto the fabric with the painted side down, and place paper towels or a thin cloth on top. Use the sponge roller to transfer the fabric paint from the twig to the cloth, making sure to roll over all leaves. Gently lift the towel and twig off the fabric to reveal the print. Repeat this process, alternating the twigs and colors of paint, until you complete your design. Allow the paint to dry for the amount of time the manufacturer recommends.

LEAF NAPKINS

These printed napkins are the perfect accessory for your leaf-printed tablecloth. The lilac-colored paint provides a nice contrast to the overall green color scheme. The vein structures of individual leaves are on full display here, testimony to the brilliant design that only nature can provide.

To make the napkins, follow the tablecloth instructions, substituting single leaves for the plant or tree twigs.

WOODLAND TRAY

With its rustic good looks, this tray spruces up any table. The double bent-twig handles are quite unusual and surprisingly comfortable to use. Whether you're serving hearty country breakfasts or apres ski drinks, your treats will receive the special delivery they deserve.

It's easy to construct this tray, especially for anyone who played with toy building logs as a child. First, collect the twigs. You'll need: two sets of five long twigs for the sides; two sets of three shorter twigs for the ends; four thick twigs for the foundation; and four thin twigs for the handles. Trim all the side twigs the same length. Cut both the end and foundation twigs to the same measurement. Achieve a rougher-looking tray by leaving the tree bark on the branches, or strip off the bark for a smooth finish. Lash the twigs together with leather cord, covered wire, or coarse twine.

HERB CENTERPIECE

F resh herbs have distinct flavors that are prized by cooks. They're grown with ease in gardens, pots, and window boxes every summer. Once autumn comes, you can harvest your favorite herbs before the first frost, and transform them into a charming natural centerpiece. The silver and green foliage of this wreath looks great on a table, especially in a terra-cotta bowl. Plan your menu to include a dish that is enhanced by the addition of dried herbs, and then let your guests season their meal right from the wreath. Long after dinner is over, your herb wreath will continue to scent the entire room.

To make this wreath, start with a small vine base that fits inside your display bowl. Cut several short lengths of brown floral tape or wire to use for tying the herb stems onto the vine. Form compact bunches of fresh rosemary, sage, lavender, or any other herb. Moving in a single direction around the vine base, attach the bunches in a spiral pattern onto the wreath. Be sure to cover the stems and tape or wire of each bunch with the leaves of the next one. Remember that the herbs will shrink slightly as they dry.

CANDLE TEPEES

Twigs are bound in fascinating ways for many different reasons. Primitive baskets and temporary shelters are two examples of the types of twig assemblages that inspired these designs.

Collect assorted twigs of different colors, textures, lengths, and thicknesses. Pick just a few that you think look good together. Spread the bottom ends of the twigs to your desired tepee size, and then tightly bind the assemblage at its center with a coarse cord. Sand the bases of the twigs as needed, so the tepee sits flat and level. Tapered glass votive holders slide safely and easily into the upper level of the twig tepee. If you wish, finish adorning your twig construction with interesting vines and dried grasses. You could even hang a name card from the twigs to mark your seating arrangements, and then let your guests take the natural candleholders home as a unique party favor.

SWING INTO SPRING

Who says a table centerpiece has to rest on the table? You can make this charming wreath and suspend it above your dining spread. This arrangement is not only attractive, but also gives you more table space for place settings and, most importantly, delicious food. Buy a prefabricated wreath and add your own natural embellishments, or make one from twigs gathered from your own backyard.

Even though the twig placement in this wreath appears completely random, some preparation and forethought are required. First, sort your twigs by size, giving special consideration to length and diameter. For this project, a woven vine or wire wreath base is easiest to disguise. Once you have a base and the sorted twigs, you need a means to hold them together. Floral wire, floral tape, or a hot glue gun work well. Assemble the wreath flat on a table, as it's easier to notice any gaps that need filling, and then suspend the wreath to attach the decorations.

This basic twig wreath can stand on its own as a thing of beauty, or it can act as a foundation for further embellishment. Add fresh leaves to the twig wreath for color, and suspend small glass vases to hold fresh flower blossoms. If you wish, hang votive holders from the wreath for a candlelight dinner with added ambience. Use tea light candles in this arrangement to keep the flames low.

THE NEPALESE MATCHMAKER

Before taking root in the places we find them today, trees walked and talked, and even married…or so it's told in Nepalese folklore. Fir was the matchmaker of the forest. One spring he saw Rhododendron's dark, glossy green leaves and beautiful flowers, and he knew that there was only one tree that matched her beauty—the Alder. Fir thought they'd be the perfect match.

Fir found Alder and urged him to go visit the beautiful Rhododendron, but Alder was too absorbed in admiring his own long, straight trunk and delicate green leaves. By the time Alder visited Rhododendron, winter had arrived. She had shed all of her glorious leaves. Alder took one look at her crooked, leafless branches and swore he would never marry such an ugly tree.

Fir persuaded Alder to give Rhododendron another chance. When spring returned, Alder and Fir found Rhododendron once again dressed in her exquisite foliage and beautiful flowers. Alder knew at that moment that he could love no other tree, for she truly matched his beauty. Alder proposed immediately, but Rhododendron refused him, saying she would never marry anyone so fickle. Vexed, Alder threw himself off a cliff. As of that day, alders grow only in deep crevices and chasms.

NATIVE TWIG PLACE MATS

S erve up any dish on these splendid natural place mats, and you're sure to feel more down-to-earth. The unique texture of each twig is a feast for your eyes, and making your own set of mats is easier than you may think.

First, you'll need to collect thin twigs that are at least as long as the mats are wide, about 18 inches (45.7 cm). You don't have to limit yourself to twigs from only one kind of tree. Combine maple twigs (gray and fairly smooth) and cedar twigs (brown and textured) to provide variation. Trim all twigs to the desired length with pruning shears or a small saw. Apply a matte lacquer finish to seal the twigs and make the place mats easy to clean. Lay the twigs parallel to each other in as many rows as you wish. Select a lashing cord such as leather, twine, or heavy string. Make your first row of binding down the center of the mat, looping and securing the cord as you attach each branch. Create four more lines of lashing, two on each side of the center, to bind the twigs together.

ON THE WALL

WHEN DESIGNING YOUR WALLS, LOOK FOR OPPORTUNITIES TO USE NATURAL MATERIALS. HANGING ARTWORKS THAT INCLUDE LEAVES, TWIGS, AND STONES WILL PROPEL YOUR WALLS TO ANOTHER DIMENSION. WHETHER YOU WANT TO DISPLAY COLLECTED TREASURES, BUILD A UNIQUE FRAME, OR CREATE A GORGEOUS WALL INSTALLATION, THERE ARE MANY WONDERFUL OPTIONS FOR YOU TO CONSIDER. GET THE PICTURE?

SOPHISTICATED SHELVES

You already know that displaying natural materials on a crisp, light surface heightens their visual appeal. Now, why not take this practice one step further by formally framing the objects? This open shelving unit, a thoroughly modern take on the traditional shadow box, gives the small treasures it contains even more distinction. Arrange, and then rearrange the contents as the spirit moves you, leaving a few boxes empty so the overall appearance stays airy. The organic contours of the featured items contrast with the strong geometric lines and angles of the shelves and table below. This wall simply and successfully illustrates how to use the dynamic tension between elements to create an interesting display.

THE MOERAKI BOULDERS

Captivating and mysterious, the boulders on the coast at Moeraki in New Zealand have intrigued ancient and modern man. The native people, the Maori, have a vivid folklore tradition with several myths surrounding the creation of the boulders.

The tales have some common themes: the legendary canoe, Arai Te Uru, was in search of a precious stone when it foundered off the coast hundreds of years ago. Supplies for the long journey washed ashore and were transformed into the landscape; the hull of the great canoe became the reef, and eel baskets, gourds, or calabashes turned into the giant round boulders—some over 13 feet (4 m) in diameter. Kumara, a potato-like food, turned into the irregularly shaped stones.

Modern science has a less imaginative explanation for the Moeraki boulders. Elements in the ocean floor gradually crystallized some 60 million years ago, lime collected around these formations, and the boulders solidified. Eventually, the earth's crust moved, and the rock layer rose to the surface.

Now the boulders are still being uncovered by the sea, some washing out of the nearby cliffs during extreme weather. Thus Maori legend lives on, as the sea continues to deliver the gourds, calabashes, and kumaru from the great Arai Te Uru to this day.

SHADOW BOXING

Another unexpected twist on traditional shadow boxes, these deep wooden frames blend the rustic appeal of storage bins with a contemporary design sensibility. Hanging the boxes in a formal grid keeps the display orderly, and pulls the viewer's focus to the contents. The natural materials held within these boxes are all from the same color family, so their shapes and textures become more significant. The repetition of identical box forms builds the intensity of the display. You can change the contents of the boxes as often as you like. This is a great way to honor the season, reflect your mood, inject some color, or present a theme.

Mary Ellen Long.
Eulogy, 1998. Outdoor installation; rock, stone, and paper. Photo by artist.

NESTING
INSTINCTS

H ere's a quick and clever way to create an
intimate and relaxing space within a larger
room. As the sun moves across the sky, the
twig valance casts striking shadows on the wall, entertaining you from hour to hour and season to season.

This is an ideal project for those seeking instant gratifi-
cation. By designing the curtain as you hang it, you take
advantage of the irregularity of the twigs and create a
completely serendipitous arrangement. Gather more
twigs than you think you need to span the ceiling. (Thin
twigs are easiest to work with and allow plenty of light
into the room.) Cut a piece of lumber or narrow board
to fit the size of your space. Using small nails or tacks,
hammer each twig onto its wooden support. Vary the
lengths of the twigs at random as you form the curtain.
Mount the support behind the ceiling beam, making
sure to leave plenty of head room.

PEBBLE PAINTING

This serene modern art triptych is a beautiful focal point for the walls in any home, and, best of all, you can make it yourself. As you admire and adhere each stone one at a time, you can participate in the meditative experience of creating art.

Determine the size of the panels you need to fit your wall space. Measure, mark, and cut pieces of ¼-inch-thick (6 mm) plywood to scale. Select a light color paint, and then brush one or more layers onto the plywood to form a solid base coat for the pebbles. Individually secure the stones with a thick, viscous glue or heavy-duty epoxy. Vary the types of stones from panel to panel as shown, or use a single stone type for monochromatic panels. Consider using other plywood shapes such as squares, circles, and triangles or scaling down the whole installation to fit a smaller space.

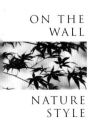

FRAMEWORK

A dried and pressed leaf has all the intriguing characteristics of a great work of art. Its composition, color, and rendering affirm the idea that the earth's greatest creative power is nature itself. A formal presentation of exceptional leaves is an ingenious way to decorate your walls—and honor Mother Nature. This project is particularly interesting because it shows balance and harmony without symmetry. Each leaf or twig is inherently unique, but instead of presenting them in a uniform manner, the designer gives each element special treatment.

The tranquil grouping is composed of one square and one rectangular wood frame, skillfully filled to complement the room's interior decor. In the upper frame, three leaf and twig collages are mounted on three different colored boards (blue, sage, and green). Separate windows are cut from a single white mat to frame the leaves. The lower frame showcases one pressed leaf atop a twig. This natural collage is mounted on a cream-colored board, and then framed with a single-layer white mat.

BRANCHING OUT

When selecting a commercial frame, your options are limited by tradition. It's also customary to contain an image within a frame's molding. This project, however, breaks away from the ordinary, showing how innovation and imagination can work together to expand the boundaries of design.

Substituting twigs for highly altered wood gives the frame a more rustic appearance, and the overall effect of the artwork is changed by the natural wood's texture and coloration. Hanging the paper, and then installing the frame at an angle, is a surprising twist. This unorthodox action breaks the viewer's conventional relationship with wall art, extending the parameters of what is to be perceived, and encouraging a more informal viewing. This presentation provides an organic sequence between fine art, its container, and your wall.

To create your own "un-frame," select four interesting twigs, and cut them to size using a miter box to saw 45° angles at each end. Join the frame together with wood glue, then staple each seam on the back of the frame with a staple gun.

XERXES AND THE SYCAMORE

While on his way to attack ancient Greece, Xerxes I, King of Persia, noticed a particularly beautiful sycamore tree. He stopped his army of 200,000 soldiers and admired the magnificent tree for three days and three nights. He watered its roots with wine and hung gold ornaments and jewelry from its branches.

Before continuing on to battle, Xerxes appointed a soldier to stand guard over the sycamore for the rest of its life. His jeweler made the likeness of the tree into an amulet, which Xerxes wore every day until he died.

DRIFTWOOD MIRROR

Mirrors, often cold to the eye, present a special decorating challenge. You can counter a mirror's steely appearance by framing it in this casual driftwood frame. Its loose lines and calm colors allow the mirror to blend more naturally into its environment. The interplay of twigs, especially their jutting corners, are just the right touch for this wall.

Each piece of driftwood has a unique, aged appearance. Create your frame from multiple layers of interlocking wood, as shown, or make a more simple statement by using a single branch for each edge. If you plan to nail your driftwood together, make sure to choose strong specimens. Not all twigs will hold up to the pressure of the hammer and may split easily.

You can alter the appearance of the driftwood with stains and sealants, or simply leave it natural to tell its own story. Left in this state, driftwood can also be a highly aromatic addition to your bathroom. Cedar in particular has a very pleasant fragrance.

Patrick Dougherty.
Crossing Over, 1996.
Maple saplings. Photo
by Dennis Cowley.

COILED VINE

The natural beauty of the vine is the star of this elegant and understated wreath. Its simplicity and integrity are not compromised by weaving or trim. Making your own coiled wreath is an entertaining project for all ages, and, if you do it yourself, you can make your wreath any size, fullness, or shape you wish.

Carry a good pair of gardening pruners with you as you set off into the woods to gather fresh vines (see page 9). Search for the longest vines possible, cut them, and then remove their leaves. Once home, make your wreath as quickly as possible. Coil the vines and place them at the bottom of a large empty container such as a trash can or tub. If the vines are too rigid, soak them in water overnight. This will make the vines pliable enough to conform to the circle. Keep the vines in this position for several weeks until they dry in this shape. Remove the vines from the container, make artistic adjustments as needed, and then loosely bind the vines together with wire. Make a hanging loop from the wire, and attach it to the top of the wreath.

FULL CIRCLE

When we look up at the sky, down at a rocky river bed, or even inside a chicken coop, circles are everywhere. This tender flowing shape, a symbol of infinity and continuity, is a source of comfort. The organic forms of these three wreaths arouse similar feelings.

Calming evergreen leaves, ornamental grasses, and pussy willows provide visual stress relief. A unique alternative to houseplants, the wreaths provide a sensational focal point in any location, and are compact enough to be hung in small spaces. All three wreaths suggest a contemporary rethinking of the media to suit the modern home. Use them alone or in groups, on or off the wall, and enjoy the timeless balance of the circle.

MORE TO MAKE WITH LEAVES

As quickly as the autumn leaves fell, our designers came up with more and more wonderful projects. We've selected a few to share with you, and hope that they'll excite your imagination.

GIFT CARD

The subtle beauty of a leaf suffuses the vellum to create a graceful adornment for a present. Choose a leaf from the spectrum of fall color when you make this card, and let the thread either complement, or contrast with, your design.

LEAFY TABLE RUNNER

What an ingenious way to decorate your table—unadorned, yet divine. Find leaves of a similar size to stitch together, cut some paper strips for a foundation, and sew; it's almost effortless. A candle or two on your table will enhance the sheen from the metallic thread; a strand of lights will add real sparkle. But don't overlook the simple beauty of this project in its natural state.

WALL DECORATIONS

The regal ginkgo enhances any wall; select only the best leaves for this display. Of course, you can use as many leaves as is appropriate for the size of your room, but the understated elegance of this assortment is striking. Let your muse lead as you consider other varieties, and mix or match them as desired.

SKELETONIZED LEAF LAMP

Create this project with relative ease, whether you choose to purchase ready-made leaves or make your own leaf skeletons. A bit of glue is all that is necessary to affix the leaves to the shade. When lighted, the leaf skeletons become translucent, adding a hint of mystery to the lamp. For a completely different effect, you could dye the leaves a dark shade, and glue them to a light lampshade.

LEAF COASTERS

You may not want to put anything on these coasters, because they're uncommonly lovely. Using copper foil tape is easy—no soldering required—so you can quickly create sets of coasters. Consider different varieties of pressed specimens (though the maple leaves are quite elegant); simply use a heavy book and absorbent paper to prepare your leaves (see page 12).

EXTRA IDEAS

■ *Add style to your serving platters by placing fresh leaves underneath hors d'oeuvres.*

■ *Place thin paper over an interesting leaf, and carefully rub with a pencil or crayon.*

■ *String leaves on ribbons and hang them in front of a window.*

■ *Adhere pressed leaves to paper for an artistic bookmark.*

TIME TO CELEBRATE

ALTHOUGH THEY'RE MOST FREQUENTLY USED TO CREATE A TRANQUIL AMBIENCE, NATURAL MATERIALS CAN BE EQUALLY EFFECTIVE FOR SETTING A FESTIVE MOOD AND CELEBRATING SEASONAL HOLIDAYS. THIS CHAPTER MOVES FROM SPRING TO SUMMER TO AUTUMN TO WINTER, PRESENTING CREATIVE DECORATING IDEAS AND PROJECTS FOR EVERY SEASON. THERE ALSO ARE UNIQUE GIFT WRAPPINGS AND CARDS TO GIVE YOUR PRESENTS NATURAL STYLE.

WARM-WEATHER
WELCOME

You'll show plenty of summer style when you hang this lush and inviting wreath on your door. Its wildness takes advantage of the season's peak when leaves and blossoms are most abundant.

For this project, you'll need a wreath base made of woven vine (purchased or homemade), small pieces of floral oasis foam, floral wire, and scissors. Evenly insert small pieces of floral oasis foam around the wreath base, filling spaces between the woven vines. Saturate the oasis with water to extend the lives of the leaves and blossoms. Cut the leaves and vines for the wreath from readily available native specimens. This makes a more natural-looking wreath that fits its environment. For their unique looks and aroma, consider incorporating vegetable leaves and herbs into your design. With their unruly textures, some weeds perfectly convey a wild image. Poke the ends of the stems into the moist oasis to keep them fresh, and tie the stems to the vines with small pieces of floral wire as needed. Once the wreath base is covered with foliage and flowers to your liking, wrap a ribbon of pliable fresh vine around the arrangement at select points.

YIN AND YANG STONES

Legend has it that unpredictable rains and frequent droughts once plagued China. Most of the time, the people simply endured it. But when the suffering was too great, a brave villager volunteered to visit the Yin and Yang stones.

A lone, tall mountain rose from the plain. On the northeast side of this mountain was a deep cave, and inside the entrance of the cave stood two stones. One of these stones, the Yin stone, was always wet and mossy. The other, called the Yang stone, was always dry and parched.

The villager would climb to the top of the mountain and enter the cave holding a whip. Whipping the Yin stone caused the rains to fall, while whipping the Yang stone caused the skies to clear.

It was a tremendous sacrifice for the villager, who was horribly damp or parched; painfully hot or cold; and unable to eat, drink, or sleep for the rest of his life. But the village—its people, their homes, their animals, and their land—would be saved by his brave actions.

ROCK SOLID

For special occasion decorating, creating luminarias from brown bags, candles, and sand is a great idea, but all too often it remains just that—an idea. The time involved in assembling the luminarias before the party, keeping them lit during the festivities, and making certain they're burning safely can be daunting. Here's a glass and stone alternative that is as quick-and-easy as it is enchanting.

The glass luminarias should fit comfortably into the corners of your stairs with plenty of room left on the run. Choose transparent vases with squared corners that are approximately the same height as the stair rise, about 6 to 7 inches (15.2 to 17.8 cm). Position an oversized votive or small pillar candle in the center of the vase; then surround the candle with stones. Use white stones, such as those shown, to reflect a lot of light. The brighter the illumination, the greater the safety of your guests as they make their way up and down the stairs.

CLASSIC GARLANDS

*Floral wreaths and garlands date back to
ancient Greece (600–146 BC), where they
were placed on the heads of heroes, on statues
of gods and goddesses, and were used to honor
the dead. At banquet tables in ancient Rome,
guests were crowned and adorned with massive
floral wreaths and garlands. As the fine arts
thrived during the Renaissance (1400–1600),
so did the buffet table come into its greatest
glory. It provided a stage for garlands, wreaths,
extravagant flowers, and, of course, an abundance of food.*

SPRING BANQUET GARLAND

Garlands—whether they're winding around
pillars or poles, draping off a table's edge,
or framing a window or door—always
seem festive, graceful, and timeless. This serving table
decoration is the strung-foliage equivalent of tuxedo
dress. It's a fun decorating project for two.

Cut a length of twine the size of the garland you wish
to make. (Twine will only support garlands made with
lightweight plant material. Heavier foliage must be
attached to a stronger base.) Clip leaves and flowers
into short pieces, approximately 3 inches (7.6 cm)
long. Assemble a bundle of flowers and foliage, secure
it with floral wire, and then fashion a hanging loop at
the end of the wire. Place the bundle on top of the
twine, and fasten it in place with wire. Create another
bundle, and position it over the stems of the first bundle. Continue making bundles of leaves and flowers
and connecting them to the twine until the garland is
complete. Lightly mist the garland with water, cover it
with moist paper towels, and then store it in a cool
place until you're ready to hang it.

GARLAND NAPKIN RINGS

Think of these gorgeous napkin rings as miniature wreaths, and you'll appreciate how easy they are to make. The profuse collection of fresh leaves in this small ring is a robust show of nature. The tiny tips of lush foliage jutting out at all angles make for an incredible display of texture, line, and color.

Cut a piece of floral wire for the base of the napkin ring, allowing extra wire at both ends. Make a hook at one end of the wire and an eye at the other. Wrap the length of wire with floral tape. Create small leaf arrangements, and then individually wire or tape them together to form a unit. Use floral tape to attach the individual leaf units to the taped wire base. Compact the foliage as you work at the same angle around the base.

Although the array of leaves on the napkin ring on the facing page is sparse, its decorative effect is no less dramatic than the heavy-clustered ring above. The silhouette of each individual leaf stands out against the clean white napkin. This napkin ring suggests the look of early Roman garlands made for holidays and royal feasts. To create this design for your own bacchanalia, follow the same process described above with a few modifications: use fewer leaves in the individual groupings; and spread the groupings further out as you attach them to the taped wire.

AUTUMN SPECTACLE

When harvest time rolls back around, forget about dusting off your old cornucopia—go out on a limb and create a new display, such as this radiant tabletop still life. It will reinvigorate the holiday season and boost your spirits, too.

To make the candlesticks, first gather a handsome group of sturdy twigs. Candleholders of different heights are much more festive and fun to arrange, so cut the twigs at various lengths ranging from 8 to 18 inches (20.3 to 45.7 cm). Saw, and then sand off all irregular edges to make both ends of each twig flat and level. On each candlestick, decide which end will be the top; then hammer a finishing nail at its center. (This provides a spike on which to impale your candle.) Use extra strength, multi-purpose glue to bond a bobeche★ to the top of each candleholder.

Finally it's time to arrange your tableau. Your twig candleholders must be stable for safety's sake. Once their placement is determined, fasten each twig in place with a small amount of museum wax. Pinch the wax off the block, and rub it between your fingers and thumb to warm it. Place the ball of wax on the bottom of each twig, and firmly set the twig onto your table. Repeat this process for each of the candlesticks, and then attach the candles. For the grand finale, add the delicious color of red apples and the intricate angles of skinny twigs to the base of your arrangement. Voila—with nature's help, you've treated yourself to a holiday makeover.

★A *bobeche* (pronounced bō bĕsh) is a round disk with a hole in the center. It fits around a taper candle and is used to catch dripping wax. Using a bobeche prevents molten wax from dripping onto your candlesticks and tables. Most bobeche are made of clear glass. If you can't locate any copper ones but still desire their look, you can color the glass bobeche with a coat of metallic spray paint.

STYLISH
WRAPPING

Distinguish your very special gift with this natural presentation. Leaf packets are a clever, attractive, and resourceful alternative to commercial wrapping papers and bows. A large and colorful leaf is the only supply required, although Spanish moss, raffia, vines, thorns, and seedpods make wonderful embellishments. The appropriate scale and dramatic appearance of tropical houseplant leaves make them the perfect choice.

Before getting started, encase your gift in Spanish moss or tissue paper for protection. Place the leaf on a flat surface with the underside facing up, and then center the gift on the leaf. To make a folded packet, tuck both sides of the leaf toward the center, fold up the leaf's stem end, fold down the leaf's point end, and then secure all four sides with a sharpened twig, a thorn, or wrapped and tied raffia. For a roll-up packet, simply roll the leaf from the stem to the point, and secure. Stuff the open ends of the leaf roll with Spanish moss to add a final flourish. Plants with floppy leaves work better for the single-leaf packet techniques. For a two-leaf packet, sandwich your gift between two identical leaves, and pin, sew, or tie the leaves closed.

SKELETONIZED
LEAF CARDS

Most people spend more creative energy composing the greeting on the interior or of a card than on the exterior image. This blank canvas, however, can be a fantastic forum for making just the right impression. These modern collages use a single skeletonized leaf, art papers, book text, mica, and beads to make a very sophisticated statement.

Place one skeletonized leaf face down on a piece of scrap paper. Using great care, brush a light layer of craft glue along the entire surface of the leaf. Apply enough glue onto the leaf surface so it will stick to the card, but not so much that the glue will be visible once dry. Press the glued side of the leaf onto a piece of decorative paper. (Dark paper is a wonderful accent to the light, delicate beauty of the skeletonized veins.) Let dry. Cut the decorative papers for the collage. Brush glue along their back surfaces, and then gently press them down onto the front side of the card. Let dry. Embellish the card with seed beads, using a beading needle and thread and a running stitch. (If you're using a stiff card stock, you may need to poke holes through the card with a regular sewing needle or awl before using the beading needle.) Adding embellishments increases the weight of the card, so you may need to add extra postage.

THE SWALLOW, THE BUMBLEBEE & THE EVERGREENS

Here is a story from Mongolian folklore: The Eternal Springs were nestled in the highest mountains. A single drop of this water could make anyone immortal, but the path to the Eternal Springs was so treacherous that only birds in flight could reach the springs.

One day, a swallow decided that the gift of immortality should be shared with the people of Mongolia. On her flight to the Eternal Springs, a bumblebee stopped the bird and asked where she was going. The swallow told the bee that she was fetching water from the Eternal Springs to give to the people.

The bumblebee was terribly jealous, because it was too cold for him to fly there. Since he couldn't become immortal, the bumblebee devised a plan to stop the swallow from delivering the water.

The swallow was carrying in her beak three drops of water from the Eternal Springs. As she flew back over the forest, the bumblebee sprang from a hiding place and stung her as hard as he could. The swallow cried out in pain, spilling the water onto a cedar, a fir, and a red bilberry tree, bestowing the gift of immortality on them; thus, these trees stay green all year long.

MAKING AN ENTRANCE

Stairways, too often slighted by decorators, are a fun field for creative play. In this scenario, a stark white wall with a modest wood tread is accented by a runner of lush foliage. Its hardy presence makes for a more inviting foyer. Not only does the runner show nature flourishing, but its rich green presence also works wonders to warm the area. Tucked into the corners, pale mini-gourds displayed in simple white bowls bestow an ethereal touch.

To create this visual treat for your home, follow the process described for the Spring Banquet Garland on page 116. Fashion the stairway swag out of any leafy greens you favor, using berry branches to add a different color and contour if you wish. Eucalyptus branches contribute tonal diversity and a delightful aroma to this runner.

RICH PROVINCIAL

At first glance, this room is nothing if not posh; a sumptuous dining environment to stimulate the senses. However, while individually evaluating its decorative elements, you'll see that nature is firmly rooted in this eclectic design.

The secret to this setting is its visual contrasts. The opulence of ruby velvet and iridescent glass are set off by the rustic charm of a simple wood table and whitewashed walls. Twig wreaths strung with mini-lights form two uncommon and dramatic chandeliers. The wreaths are tightly constructed with little space between the twigs, making a shadowy base from which the lights sparkle. Jagged artichokes displayed in cylindrical vases of polished glass, fuzzy herbs in a shiny black lacquer bowl, a vine wreath wrapped with course twine lying flat in a low metal vessel—all of these are small ways you can combine diverse materials, elevating the visual intensity of nature's bounty to harmonize within an opulent setting.

MERRY CHANDELIER

Chandeliers are unfortunately burdened with the pretense of being either ostentatious displays of crystal or shabby metal design calamities. This homemade alternative successfully dispels both notions. Again, it's nature to the rescue, this time in the form of an arresting group of overlapping twigs.

A quick-and-easy drape of sparkling mini-lights highlights the linear qualities of the twigs without overpowering them. Mini-lights, once exclusively hung for the holidays, have shed their seasonal trappings to become tasteful year-round. A quick, inexpensive, and low-maintenance decorating solution, mini-lights produce glowing effects with very little effort. To create ambience, they're a great substitute for candles. This one-of-a-kind lighting fixture flatters any occasion, whether it's a big party or an intimate get-together.

To create this chandelier, choose 10 to 12 twigs, and cluster them around a mini-light strand. Tightly arrange the bottom ends of the twigs to encircle and disguise the wire. (The cords on most mini-lights are green, but, for this project, use a strand with a white cord so it's concealed as much as possible.) Leave the cord's *lead*, or distance between its plug and first bulb, free to be run to an electrical outlet or extension cord. Wrap one end of heavy-duty twine around the arrangement, make a tight knot, and then run the other end of the twine through a hook in the ceiling, over a rafter, or other hanging device. Pull the cord to adjust the height of the light fixture to the desired level, and secure. Evenly string the mini-light strand around the twig chandelier. The spacing of the bulbs on the cord, which can vary considerably, affects the way the lights look when they're displayed. For stability, use small pieces of wire or clear monofilament to fasten the cord to the twigs in several points. Plug in your new lighting feature, and marvel at the magic.

Mari Marks Fleming. *Intervals, #3*, 2001.
Beeswax, pigment, and ginkgo leaves.
Photo by Don Felton.

MANTEL HARMONY

For a fresh new look, why not incorporate stones into your seasonal decorating? The dark green pine is not only fragrant but also adds textural contrast to this mantle arrangement. Just as you long to caress the smooth stones, you'll also want to stroke the short, pointed pine needles. The two colors of deep pine and light stone really come alive with the addition of vermilion column candles. To create a harmonious arrangement, choose candles that are comparable in diameter to the stones. These two elements will then carry the same visual weight. The pine boughs are so darkly colored that despite their small stature they too carry similar weight. Vary the candle heights to suit the organic nature of the design. You may even want to select fragranced candles, such as cranberry or cinnamon spice, to enhance the pine and celebrate the spirit of the season.

WINTER TWIG SWAG

Create this handsome and unusual swag from tightly grouped twigs. It's a wonderful project for you to make with family and friends for the holidays. Bundle everyone up in their warm winter gear, grab a basket, and strike out into the woods to find the perfect twigs and pinecones.

After you've gathered an ample supply and are back at home, divide the twigs into small groups. Cut a length of rope or wire to the size desired for your swag foundation line. Surround the end of the line with one group of twigs; then tightly twist a small length of wire around one end of the bundle to secure. Repeat this process down the length of the foundation line, making sure to overlap each new bundle over the previously twisted wire.

Once you've created the basic twig garland, you can embellish it any way you like. A swath of pinecones brings new shapes and textures to your swag while remaining within the same color palette. Attach the pinecones with the same wire you used for the twigs. You can twist the pinecone wire around either the swag foundation line or around a single branch. Once the swag is installed on your mantel, hang other decorative flourishes onto the twigs with small metal ornament hooks.

FANCIFUL FERN WREATH

If carefree elegance is the mood you'd like to set for your holiday entertaining, then creating this enchanting wreath might be a good place to start. It combines lacy fern fronds with dried baby's breath and feathers for a unique ethereal appearance and can be constructed with very little effort.

PREPARING THE MATERIALS

You'll need a foam base for your wreath foundation and an ample supply of floral picks. Select silver-blue tone fern fronds for your wreath, or mist a thin coat of metallic spray paint onto ordinary fronds. (If you choose to spray paint your fern, spray large individual leaves at the same time. Place these on top of cloth napkins, as shown in the photo, or informally scatter them down the center of the tablecloth.) Lay the foam wreath base flat on a work table. Tie three separate lengths of hanging cord to the base at equal points around its circumference.

Securely knot the cords and make sure they are long enough to reach a hanger. Cut the greenery to the desired lengths.

ASSEMBLING THE WREATH

Begin attaching the fern fronds one at a time by pushing a floral pick over each stem and securing it into the foam base. First, cover the wreath base with long fern fronds; then fill in with smaller cuttings to disguise the foam. Once the wreath looks full, add decorative accents such as dried baby's breath and feathers as desired. To make your suspended wreath a source of illumination for your table, use decorative wire to attach hanging votive holders to the foam base. Hang the votive holders far enough down from the wreath so that the burning candles will not be a fire hazard, and never leave the candles unattended when lit.

Mary Ellen Long. *Leaf Page: Nelson, New England,* 2001. Collage with thorns. Photo by artist.

CRYSTAL VISION

For those with aristocratic tastes, a light spray of white paint can transform an ordinary branch from an earthy accessory to an opulent delight. If you don't happen to have any extra chandelier prisms hanging around, or you choose not to take apart a family heirloom, don't worry. Chances are good that you'll find a wide variety of prisms for sale at antique malls, flea markets, or hardware restoration centers. Attach these wonderful reflectors onto your painted twigs with metal ornament hooks as shown, or with any festive ribbon or thread you desire. Chandelier prisms are often heavy, so affix the hooks at strong points on the twig. Use a few well-placed staples or nails to keep the decoration in place on your mantle.

Mary Ellen Long. *Costa Rica Leaves,* 2000.
Outdoor installation; leaf collage. Photo by artist.

WARDING TREES

Some trees have been associated with superstition since ancient times.

Because evil spirits couldn't pass under birch branches, families in Russia were protected from misfortune by hanging them above the front entrance to their property.

In Sicily, elder branches were used to drive out serpents and ward off thieves. (Some say that St. Patrick drove the serpents out of Ireland with a staff of elder wood.)

In Germany, Walpurgis Night on April 30 signaled the end of the witching season. Rowan branches were hung all over the house to protect the family and its belongings from evil spirits during their last night of devilment.

The yew has been associated with the dead since ancient times. Yew trees are found in graveyards throughout Europe, planted to guard the sleep of the dead. It was widely believed that the spirits of the dead would send plagues of misfortune onto a community if their yew trees were cut down.

In some parts of England, finding an ash leaf by chance was good luck. If the finder kept the leaf, success and happiness would follow. But the ash leaf had to be found—plucking it off the branch guaranteed a lifetime of bad luck.

CELESTIAL JUBILEE

Cutting and decorating an evergreen tree is a winter holiday tradition. It's such an time-honored ritual that few even consider other options. If you're inspired to restyle your celebrations, however, these suspended vine wreaths make an artful and elegant alternative. You can even hang the same tree-trimming ornaments from the wreaths, using standard wire hooks. This is an eco-friendly project that's reusable from season to season. You can also alter the wreath's embellishments for use on other occasions.

These wreaths are particularly impressive because of their volume. They're unusually thick and full. Collect a substantial supply of vines in various sizes in order to replicate their style. In the winter, vines go dormant, so once you've got your stash home, you'll need to submerge them in water for 12 to 24 hours so they'll be pliable. Once you're ready to create your wreaths, follow the process described on page 84 for Swing into Spring.

GALLERY

Patrick Dougherty.
Owache, 1999.
Mixed hardwood saplings.
Photo by Larry Gregory.

Lynne Hull. *Scatter Hydroglyph,* 1986.
Stone. Photo by artist.

Patrick Dougherty. *Be It Ever So Humble,* 1999.
Maple saplings. Photo by Star Kotowski.

Mary Ellen Long.
Leaf Book, 2000.
Book sculpture;
leaves and thread.
Photo by artist.

R. G. Solbert. *Y Is Why, 1999.* Stained and oiled hardwoods. Photo by artist.

Lynne Hull. *Observation Screen from Giraffe Center Project*, 1994. Lantana vine. Photo by artist.

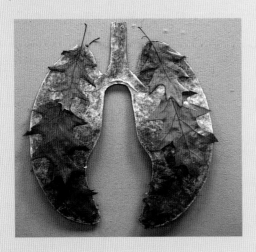

R. G. Solbert. *Breath,* 2001. Formed mica and preserved oak leaves. Photo by artist.

Bill Botzow, *Wedge,* 1997. Leaves and resin on plywood. Photo by artist.

Gyöngy Laky. *Protest: Naught for Naught,* 2000. Various orchard prunings and screws. Photo by artist.

Gyöngy Laky. *Oll Korrect,* 1998. Apricot prunings, pine molding, and vinyl coated steel nails. Photo by Tom Grotta.

Roy F. Staab. *Liquid Lens,* 1998. White stones underwater. Photo by artist.

Sylvia Benitez Stewart. *Beneath the Bark: Under Leaf and Log Installation,* Wave Hill Bronx, NY, Part 3: Among the Trees, 2000. Photo by artist.

Ueno Masao. *Camellia and Fern,* 2000. Fallen camellia and woven fern. Photo by artist.

Roy F. Staab. *Goose Cross Glowing,* 2001. Reeds. Photo by artist.

Roy F. Staab. *Aftertide Meridian,* 1998. Stones. Photo by artist.

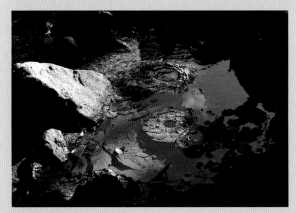

Ueno Masao. *Pagoda of Leaves,* 1994. Woven leaves. Photo by artist.

Bill and Ruth Botzow. *Martes Martes: A Habitat Enhancing Sculpture for the American Marten,* 2001. Debarked maple sticks filled with sorted forest material. Photo by Bill Botzow.

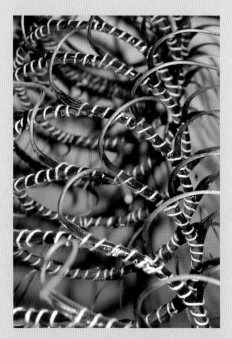

Christine Rose McMillan. *Banded Gyre (biodiversity I),* detail, 2000. Xanthorrhoea leaf bases, string, and metal spiral. Photo by artist.

INDEX

INDEX OF GALLERY ARTISTS

ACKNOWLEDGMENTS

Many thanks to: Dana Irwin, Sara and Gerald Le Van, Rick Morris, Rob Pulleyn, Olivier Rollin, Heather Spencer and Charles Murray, Carol Stangler, Terry Taylor, Nicole Tuggle, Keith and Wendy Wright, and The Planet Earth Image Gallery at http://gugus.com.